'Puppy Love'
by Bark Busters

A COMMONSENSE GUIDE TO PUPPY SELECTION, REARING AND EARLY EDUCATION.

First published in Australia 2002 by Sylvia Wilson and Danny Wilson.

Edited and reprinted in the United States 2005.

Address all enquiries to:

www.barkbusters.com.au

1800-067-710

Danny and Sylvia Wilson

Contents

Dedication 3

Foreword 4

About the Authors 7

About Bark Busters 10

Introduction 11

Chapter 1 | Pick of the Litter Bringing a New Puppy Home 13

Chapter 2 | The Early Days 22

Chapter 3 | Understanding Your Puppy 32

Chapter 4 | The Thinking Behind Bark Busters Training 37

Chapter 5 | Steps to Having a Well-Behaved Puppy 43

Chapter 6 | The Proper Way to Educate a Puppy 53

Chapter 7 | Toilet Training 59

Chapter 8 | Early Basic Education 67

Chapter 9 | Solving Common Problems 75

Chapter 10 | Children and Your Puppy 81

Chapter 11 | Visitors and Your Puppy 88

Chapter 12 | Grooming Your Puppy 91

Chapter 13 | Socializing Your Puppy 93

Chapter 14 | Pack Mentality vs Socialization 97

Chapter 15 | Special Tips for Puppy Owners 107

Chapter 16 | Summing Up 109

Chapter 17 | Bark Busters 50 Most Popular Breeds 112

Dedication

This book is dedicated to all the dogs that shared our lives, gave us endless amounts of joy, and have now passed on. These wonderful creatures taught us so much about the canine world.

It is because of our love for and appreciation of all dogs, especially puppies, that we have written this book.

Dedicated To

Diesel the Rottweiler. The day we rescued Diesel was one of the best days of our lives. He died way too early when his life was cut short by a snake bite on 11 September 2011.

We miss him every day.

Foreword
by Dr. Byron J S de la Navarre, DVM

We have been working with Bark Busters Dog Training for many years. They have a fantastic variety of training programs able to suit any situation. There are several great aspects of Bark Busters that make them our favorite Chicago Dog Training group.

They have the ability to meet with our clients in any situation/location: in the home, at the park, in a group or one on one, with just the client's dogs or also involving their own dogs to help resolve dog to dog behavioural problems.

The Bark Busters wonderful team in Chicago brings a wealth of knowledge and ideas on how to handle all behavioural issues combined with great enthusiasm and endless patience. The Bark Busters trainers are committed to resolving any behavioural problems – no matter how long it takes and how often therapy is required.

Although the Bark Busters trainers have a solid foundation of knowledge and methodology, they themselves continue to learn and attend training sessions to keep their therapy techniques on the cutting edge. They have also conducted in-hospital teaching/behavioural training sessions for our staff.

Many of us at Animal House have used them for our own dogs and have been able to see firsthand how well they work, not only with our dogs, but also with us as clients. Their expertise has helped us immensely by teaching us what they know about dog behaviour and giving us some basic training tools to then pass on to our clients.

All dog owners can benefit from Bark Busters training techniques and guidance. This is why we routinely refer our clients with new puppies to them, as we feel that early education and explanation of proper and sensible socialisation is key to allowing a dog to grow into a happy and psychologically healthy member of the family/pack.

The Bark Busters Team is continually coming up with new ideas to better serve our clients. They have made themselves available 24/7 not only to us, but also to our clients. They have put together an excellent website that serves as a great resource for information as well as another avenue to contact them and to share ideas on a national level. Along with working with individual clients, knowing how important socialisation is to dogs, they have also organized group meetings and training sessions. There does not appear to be anything they would not do to try and resolve any behavioural problem that we or our clients may encounter.

It is for this reason, and all other reasons listed above, that we have and will continue to refer to the Bark Busters Dog Training Team as our number one source/resource for dog behavioural training and therapy.

If you have any questions – please contact me.

Sincerely, Byron de la Navarre, D.V.M.

Dr. Byron J.S. de la Navarre, D.V.M.

Past-President, Association of Reptilian & Amphibian Veterinarians (ARAV)

Co-Director, Midwest Exotic Seminars (MEPS)

Secretary, Chicago Veterinary Emergency & Specialty Centre (CVESC)

Past-President, Chicago Veterinary Medical Association (CVMA)

Illinois State Liaison, Association of Avian Veterinarians (AAV)

Chairperson, Chicago Herpetological Society (CHS)

Conservation & Research Committee

Past-Chairperson/Member, Member Services Committee (AVMA)

Animal House of Chicago

Complete Veterinary Care Inc

2752 West Lawrence Avenue, Chicago, Illinois. 60625

Tel: (773) 878 8002. Fax: (773) 878 0546

Email: exotxdr@aol.com

About the Authors
Sylvia Wilson

Sylvia began dog training at an early age. Her love of puppies and their early education came natural to her and there was always a puppy or dog in her life growing up that needed her attention.

At age 15, she adopted a German Shepherd puppy that she named Monty. Monty, with Sylvia's guidance, went on to become one of the first dogs in Australia to become an Obedience Champion.

Her early years in dog training were spent as Chief Instructor of the Shoalhaven Training Club where she pioneered her first "Difficult Dog Program". This program was designed for dogs deemed untrainable or too vicious to handle. The program gained enormous interest from desperate dog owners who previously had nowhere to turn and who were shunned by the clubs who lacked the ability to deal with difficult dogs. The program ran for six years and saved many dogs from euthanasia.

Sylvia went on to manage an RSPCA shelter for ten years where she again introduced her Difficult Dog Program and normal obedience training, achieving outstanding results.

Sylvia left the RSPCA in 1989 to form her own company, Who Ya Gonna Call Bark Busters, with her husband, Danny Wilson.

The research and knowledge gained from running the Difficult Dog Program and working closely with puppies, formed part of the basis for the Bark Busters system as it is known today.

Bark Busters is now the largest dog training company of its kind in the world with offices throughout Australia, Canada, Japan, New Zealand, United Kingdom, United States, and Spain.

Danny Wilson

Danny began his dog training career in the United Kingdom where, as a child, he had a natural ability to handle dogs that were deemed untrainable or vicious. During his early years as a child growing up in the northeast of England, he worked closely with a country vet who took him on his visits to farms. He spent many hours learning how the sheep farmers trained their puppies to herd sheep and learning from some of the most experienced sheep dog handlers in the district.

He later became very interested in canine behavioural issues and how dogs from different countries, when relocated, were able to communicate with each other. It was obvious they all spoke the same language, regardless of what language their owners spoke.

Danny met Sylvia at the RSPCA when he moved back to Australia (the country of his birth) in 1983.

About Bark Busters

Bark Busters began operations in 1989 in Wollongong, New South Wales, after Sylvia Wilson left the RSPCA. They both knew that they understood the root of behavioural problems and how to communicate to dogs to help their owners with their rehabilitation and early education. Determined to do something, they know would save the lives of dogs, Sylvia, and her husband Danny, formed Bark Busters.

For many years independently, the couple had studied the way dogs communicated and related to each other. At the dog shelter where Sylvia worked, they had also observed firsthand how puppies suffered from stress when taken out of their natural environment and brought to the shelter, Sylvia and Danny decided there was a need for a home dog-training service and canine education program, where the owner was always present, and the environment was the least stressful for the puppy or dog. This would be the optimum situation for education.

In 1989, Sylvia and Danny started the first of its kind, home dog-training company in Australia, and soon began receiving calls from all over Australia. From a humble beginning as a husband-and-wife operation, the company has now expanded throughout Australia to New Zealand, the United Kingdom, the United States, Canada, Japan, and Spain.

Introduction

This book is designed to make owning a puppy the loving pleasure it should be. It is a guide for prospective and current puppy owners to help them understand the way puppies learn and communicate, how they think, and how to rear a well-adjusted loving pet.

Puppy Love by Bark Busters ® A Common Sense Guide to Puppy Selection Rearing and Early Education, authors Sylvia and Danny Wilson, also explains why some puppies are shy and withdrawn, while others are social butterflies. The book explores everything you need to know and do before acquiring a new puppy. It explains how to choose one with a compatible temperament. This book is also an invaluable resource for people who already have a puppy.

In a very practical way, *Puppy Love* by Bark Busters ® A Common Sense Guide to Puppy Selection Rearing and Early Education takes you through puppy selection, the early days of bringing a puppy home, explaining how to help settle your puppy into its new environment, and how to cope with first night anxiety.

You will learn how to housebreak, entertain, exercise, and nurture your puppy, how to correctly introduce it to visitors and how to socialize it. The book also offers simple tips on puppy education.

The book contains tips for owners on how to communicate with deaf and visually impaired puppies, as well as guidance for expectant parents and senior citizens.

At Bark Busters we have a special affinity with puppies and a complete understanding of their needs. This knowledge has been developed over many years of working with hundreds of thousands of canines.

We see firsthand the problems that can occur when people are not fully armed with the correct information on how best to socialize, educate, and rear a puppy.

It is our aim to foster good puppy management and careful guidance to ensure that all puppies receive understanding, early basic education, and the best care ever.

Chapter 1

Pick of the Litter-Bringing a New Puppy Home

Things you Need to Know

Selecting the right pup for your circumstances is of great importance if you want to have an adult dog that is easy to educate and manage. A dog that has an undesirable temperament, personality and incompatible traits can create many headaches for its owner, now, and in the future.

A puppy should be no younger than eight weeks – and preferable between eight to twelve weeks of age – before being separated from its mother.

Younger than eight weeks is too early because the puppy will miss out on important guidance and social interaction with its mother and littermates. Even though the puppy might have been weaned at five weeks of age, it is still better to let it stay with its mother for those extra weeks to hone its natural canine social skills.

Some breeders will hold onto puppies for up to three months so that they have a better idea of which pup to keep for show purposes. This practice is generally acceptable unless the puppy that is kept back is not socialized correctly during that period.

Reputable breeders will have already socialized your puppy, and the puppy might even have attended a dog show or two.

All of these issues must be considered when you are thinking of getting a puppy, because early education is important. A puppy left to its own devices for hours will not receive the education required to mold it into a well-adjusted adult. Statistics show that 85% of puppy buyers buy on impulse. This causes problems because they are ill-prepared.

Acquiring Your New Puppy

Where you get your puppy is just about as important as the breed you choose. A poorly bred puppy may cost you dearly and may create much heartache, whereas most reputable breeders and reputable pet shops will stand by their puppies, and it will be understanding if problems arise.

Once you are confident that you know which breed and personality are right for you, you will need to find the right place to acquire your puppy, and the puppy with the right personality.

Puppy Breeders

A reputable breeder is one way to go, especially if you want a purebred dog of known ancestry.

Reputable breeders breed for temperament as well as physical attributes. They will be able to point you to the puppy with the right personality for you.

Some breeders sell their puppies to select pet stores. If you decide to purchase your puppy from a pet store, choose a store that is reputable, does not sell puppies coming from 'puppy farms', and offers a health guarantee.

Animal Shelters

If you are not particular about breed or ancestry and just want a little cuddly puppy; consider an animal shelter. Animal shelters sometimes have purebred puppies available, although these generally find homes quickly.

Crossbreeds are just as adorable as purebreds. They are generally 10 times hardier and less prone to the common hereditary faults of their purebred cousins. Many shelters 'temperament test' puppies before placing them up for adoption.

Choosing a Breed to Suit Your Personality

Investigate the breed that best suits your needs. Make sure you really know what the grown-up version of the puppy is like. Consider the purpose for which that breed was originally bred. Research the breed carefully and check out our list of Bark Busters 50 Most Popular Breeds in Chapter 17.

Think carefully about your circumstances and lifestyle. There are some very informative books available that can help you choose the right breed for you.

Dr. Bruce Fogle's book, 'Dogs', published by Dorling and Kinderley, profiles hundreds of breeds of dogs, highlighting their breed traits.

The Bark Busters website, www.barkbusters.com., lists many popular breeds. It details how much time and energy is required of the owners.

Selecting the Right Puppy for You

When we are asked to select a puppy from a litter, we first view all of the puppies together. We watch them run and play, and we focus on the differences in the body language of each pup as it interacts with the others.

This gives us an indication as to where each pup fits in the pecking order. The puppies that are most confident will display bossy behaviour (standing over the others and snapping to control), and the less confident ones will act more submissive (rolling over or lowering their height).

The pup that takes a little bit longer to approach you or tries to run away might be too timid for a family situation. This type of puppy might be best in a situation where there is only one or two in the family. With special care, and proper gentle education, it will become a very acceptable companion.

The pup that barks at you, refuses to approach you, or responds by crouching down when you reach out, is very fearful. This is not the most desirable temperament. The pup is likely to become the type of dog that barks at everything that moves, which could cause problems for the uninitiated dog owner (especially if you live in an apartment or condo).

See if you can carefully lift and hold each pup in your arms. A pup that sits still is far more acceptable for a person of soft nature than a pup that squirms and bites at the hands.

Be sure you know what temperament you want in a puppy and choose accordingly. Do not choose a timid type of personality if you have an outgoing, confident personality. Likewise, don't choose the confident type of puppy if you are of a very soft nature and want a dog that is easy to educate.

Do not, for any reason, take home the very frightened puppy sitting in the corner alone. It is sitting alone for a good reason and, more than likely, it will be the puppy that grows into an adult dog that fears the world.

Personality and Lifestyle

Be sure to select a breed of dog that will suit your lifestyle and personality because choosing a breed that is wrong for you could be disastrous.

For example, a frail, docile person would find a large-breed dog difficult to control.

Similarly, a very active small breed might prove to be too much, especially if the breed is boisterous and hyperactive and especially if you live in an apartment or condo.

Check out our selection of the list of Bark Busters 50 Most Popular Breeds in Chapter 17.

One Puppy or Two?

We are often asked whether two puppies should be purchased, and our answer is always the same, *"only if you genuinely want two dogs."* Otherwise, you will have twice the work and two pups are not going to be any more content than one.

Some pups just want their mother; even their littermate cannot replace that need, two puppies from the same litter can prove problematic.

Two puppies from the same litter can prove problematic. Two pups from the same litter as they grow, may have serious fights to establish superiority. This is less dramatic if the two pups are male and female because the male normally will back down and allow the female to rule. Nevertheless, we do get calls where this has not been the case, especially if the female is overly domineering and the male becomes fearful. This personality combination can lead to fights.

There are cases in which a male dog is also very assertive and refuses to back down, regardless of how persistent the other dog is and whether or not it is female. Fortunately, this is not common.

Two puppies of the same sex can be a worse combination, and even neutering or spaying may not alleviate the squabbling. We deal with many cases in which two males, or two females are fighting; we refer to this as 'sibling rivalry.' However, we do know of thousands of same (six) pairings that work amazingly well.

If you do decide to buy two puppies from the same litter, it might be wise to choose a male and female, providing you intend to have them both desexed. See the section entitled, Benefits of Desexing in Chapter 2.

It is not a good idea to select a small-breed puppy and a large-breed puppy. If they start squabbling, the size difference could present difficulties.

Another option would be to buy a dog and a kitten at the same time. They make great mates at this time of lift and the kitten may house-train the puppy automatically. This is because, in most cases, the puppy will follow the good toilet habits of the kitten and use the litter tray. They will remain great mates. Remember, though, that puppies and kittens have different dietary issues, and you must cater for this.

Puppy Proofing Your Home

Puppies are adventurous and can get into areas you would never imagine. They will chew and carry around everything they find. Be sure that there are no dangerous items lying around in your home, just the way you would if you had a two-year old child. Prevent access to dangers such as live electrical cables, cleaning fluids, old batteries, pesticides, sharp objects, broken glass, or tins.

Give your puppy safe toys to entertain it. Provide shade, adequate shelter, and plenty of fresh water. The toys we recommend are GameChanger ® Brand Toys.

Proper Management of Your Puppy

The proper management and care of a puppy is important and not to be attempted lightly. Rearing a puppy is a big responsibility and, like a baby, a puppy requires constant attention.

It needs to be fed several times a day and be on the correct diet, your understanding, shelter, education, and entertainment.

If you cannot provide this care and attention around the clock, you should seriously consider choosing a full-grown dog instead of a puppy.

Six Steps to Acquiring a New Puppy

1. Check your home out. Is it dog friendly?

2. Know which breed is right for you. Do your homework first. Check out the Bark Busters website, www.barkbusters.com.

3. Choose only reputable breeders or reputable pet shops. Also check out animal shelters and dog rescue groups. Consult veterinarians or select dogs from local animal shelters.

4. Consider your own personality and choose accordingly.

5. Follow the above rules for selecting the right temperament to fit your lifestyle.

6. Remember, the shelters, dog rescue groups, breeders and pet shops should know their puppies. Ask them to assist you with the right selection for your personality and lifestyle.

Chapter 2

The Early Days

Settling In

Bring your new puppy home early in the day so that it has the whole day to settle in. During the day, your puppy will become tired and want to sleep. Try to ensure that it falls asleep in the same place you have selected for it to sleep during the night.

By watching the puppy closely when you first bring it home, you will be able to see when it becomes tired. Then you can place it in its intended bed.

Sleeping Quarters

A covered crate or small wire cage is the best bed and will also provide a good start for toilet training. Initially, leave the cage door open until the puppy learns to trust its new environment (a strong, high-sided cardboard box can be used as a short-term alternative).

By evening, the puppy will have established a safe haven for itself and will feel more comfortable when left alone at night in its closed crate.

Be aware that if you choose a crate, cage, or box for your puppy, you might need to get up a couple of times during the night to let it out to toilet unless your cage is large enough to include a toilet area. Despite the inconvenience, it is worth the effort and will pay dividends later. It is also important to let your puppy walk to the toilet area rather than you carrying it there.

You don't want your puppy to associate the toilet as a place it will go after having to be picked up. You need it to find its own way eventually – so teach it to find its own way.

In general, we have found that if you ensure that the puppy goes to the toilet before you put it to bed for the night, it will last most of the night. It is wise to place your puppy in its sleeping place at least an hour before you go to bed yourself. Position plenty of soft, warm bedding in the puppy's bed and then leave the puppy along, allowing it time to settle before you go to bed.

Soft Toys

All puppies will suffer stress when taken away from their mother and littermates, so it is helpful to have a soft toy for your puppy to cuddle up to. If possible, rub the soft toy over the mother's fur to collect her scent. A hot water bottle or heating pad with provide warmth and comfort.

Bedtime

Regardless of how much effort you expend in doing the right thing and preparing for your puppy, you will experience a certain amount of crying from the pup during the first few days.

When this occurs, check on your puppy to ensure that it is not stuck or hurt. Once you are convinced that it is safe, clap your hands loudly and growl "Bah!" You are letting your puppy know that you are close by, but that you do not approve of its behaviour.

This will settle puppies far more quickly than ignoring the crying. Ignoring it only leads the puppy to believe it has been abandoned, and its screams may escalate to a pitch that you cannot ignore.

Never rush to the pup to console it. If you do, you will be doing this for the rest of its life. Although it is 'tough love', going through the separation and settling-in period, it is better to do it at this stage rather than later when you have to go out and leave your puppy at home. If done later, the separation for the puppy will be worse; you won't be close by to growl your displeasure and it may create major separation anxiety problems as the pup now feels abandoned.

Case History

Czar the Great Dane was found in a shoebox as an orphaned three-week-old puppy. From the day his owner found him, she could not bring herself ever to leave him alone.

At the time, this did not present a big problem because he was very tiny and needed constant care. His owner was also lucky enough to be able to take him to work.

As he grew and grew, however, the problem became more serious. It became difficult to take him everywhere and the owner needed to hire dog sitters.

Czar grew very large and extremely dependent on his owner. If she went out without him, he would crash through windows to follow her. This placed a huge emotional burden on his owner, who loved him dearly but sometimes needed her own space.

Czar's diet was altered to provide a calming effect and to assist with weight. Bark Busters therapy was commenced promptly.

The therapy consisted of establishing leadership, and reassuring Czar that whenever his owner left, she would return. The education process began with short separation periods that were gradually extended until czar was no longer concerned about his owner leaving.

Although problems like this can be remedied by Bark Busters, it is easier to prevent the problem from occurring in the first place. Prevention is always better than a cure.

A puppy that is constantly with its owner and has every demand met, will develop anxiety when the owner tries to leave it alone. It will demand that the owner returns immediately and will become very stressed when they don't.

Nutrition

Puppies need good, natural nutrition, especially at this stage of life. An unbalanced or inadequate diet will create an unhappy and stressed puppy. When you collect your puppy, most shelters, breeders and pet shops will supply the details of the puppy's diet.

If you feel your puppy has not been on the right diet, do not make sudden changes. A sudden diet change could cause stomach problems and diarrhea. Any change of diet must be gradual.

Bark Busters recommends a diet that is low in carbohydrates, free from coloring and preservatives. Do not ever feed your puppy or dog and rice or pasta in addition to its prepared food. This will only make your pet hyperactive and too difficult to control. We do urge you to conduct your own investigation and do your homework on which diet is best for your dog's needs.

Make sure you research all of the information available before deciding on what is best for your puppy and consult your veterinarian.

Safety First

Your puppy will need a safe environment in which to play and exercise, preferably one with sunlight and fresh air. We realize this is not always possible, as some pet owners live in high-rise apartments.

Wherever you choose to keep your puppy, make sure it is a safe environment, free from broken glass, poisons, electrical cables, and toxic plants.

Entertainment

Like a child, a puppy needs entertainment. Unlike a child, however, it cannot read books or watch television, so entertainment must always be provided.

One of the toys we recommend, the GameChanger ® which come in several sizes are virtually indestructible and can provide a puppy with hours of fun. Fill the GameChanger ® with good quality dry food that is low in carbohydrates and free from harmful colofavrings and preservatives.

This canine toy will remain your dog's favorite toy of all time. You can purchase in from your Bark Busters therapist.

Another popular with dogs is the strong and sturdy Kong. There are many designs and varying options available. Speak to your local Bark Busters therapist for details.

Warning

If living in an area where wasps are prevalent, be wary of leaving fresh meat out for your puppy. Wasps have been known to land on meat and meaty bones, resulting in the unsuspecting puppy or dog coming along to eat the bone with the wasp still on the meat. Several puppies and dogs have been bitten on the tongue that way resulting in a very painful death.

Be careful not to keep toys or playthings that might prove detrimental to your puppy's health or well-being. Items such as hanging toys that encourage the puppy to leap and jump are definitely not suitable. A puppy's growing bones are soft and not yet fully developed. This constant leaping and landing can cause skeletal alignment problems and may result in the need for a doggy chiropractor to rectify the problem.

Other items that can also present problems for your puppy are plastic bottles. Some over-exuberant pups chew these items, resulting in fragments that can lodge in the gums or stomach with disastrous results.

Ball Safety

Balls also can prove dangerous if they are small enough to be swallowed by the pup. We have heard many horror stories from vets who performed operations on dogs and puppies to remove balls that had been swallowed.

Stick Safety

Sticks are very dangerous. We have heard equally disturbing stories about dogs and puppies that have swallowed sticks which then became lodged under the dog's tongue. When thrown, sticks can land poking into the ground. An exuberant puppy or dog could pounce on the upright stick, causing serious injury. A better choice would be to use a plastic dumbbell, available from pet outlets.

Vaccinations, Microchips, and WaggTagg™

All puppies need vaccinating against rabies, distemper, parvo virus, and kennel cough. There are two strains of kennel cough your puppy must be immunized against. Ensure that you keep all certificates issued by the vent, as boarding kennels need proof of vaccination before you leave your dog.

In some countries a microchip is no mandatory by law. The tiny microchip is implanted under the skin, enabling the puppy to be identified by a scanning process.

Speak to you Bark Busters therapist WaggTagg™ - another option to protect your dog or check out www.WaggTagg.com.

Only authorized people can access this information. If your puppy is lost or stolen, the information on the microchip will help to get your puppy returned to you.

Registration

In most countries it is mandatory to register your dog with the local authorities. Check with your local authorities on the legalities of owning a dog and the registration process.

The Benefits of Desexing (Neutering/Spaying)

In western society, desexing (neutering/spaying) is very popular and widely recommended as a good way to solve some behavioural problems such as aggression, biting, and anti-social behaviour.

There are good reasons for desexing both male and female dogs.

Males

Male dogs will do less marking (urinating on further, for example) if desexed (neutered) at an early age. Early desexing results in deleted testosterone levels and the dog will be less likely to develop aggressive tendencies towards their owners, other male dogs, and people. Speak to our vet about desexing options.

The early desexing of a male dog usually results in the dog becoming calmer, easier to control, and in general, easier to manage.

Desexing does not change the dog's temperament or its personality, as some people mistakenly believe. Nor does desexing make a dog fat. Dogs become fat because they are overfed. Desexing may increase the dog's interest in food, but if the dog's diet is carefully monitored, the dog should remain lean. All of our dogs were desexed, and we are yet to have a dog with a weight problem because we carefully monitor the amount of food we feed them.

Desexing a male dog that is displaying aggression towards other male dogs can sometimes solve the problem, providing it is a display of dominant aggression. However, if the aggression is caused because the dog was attacked by another dog, or because of its fear of other dogs, then desexing will have little effect. The dog still should be desexed as a matter of course because it will make the dog easier for the owner to control.

Female

Desexing (spaying) female dogs is generally more accepted by the public and eliminates the production of unwanted litters. It makes sense that both males and females should be desexed unless, of course, you are a registered breeder.

Very destructive, or out of control, female dogs can sometimes have their behaviour modified simply by spaying them.

Chapter 3

Understanding Your Puppy

What is a Puppy?

We believe that if the right steps are carefully followed with respect to educating a dog, a puppy is really a blank canvas from which a wonderful, loyal, trouble-free pet can be created.

In other words, a puppy is a pure, unspoiled infant. How we go about turning this unspoiled creature into a well-adjusted adult will be determined by how careful and precise we are when we commence its education and nurturing.

Puppies can be traumatized easily. Any type of education must be fair and just and must in no way traumatize the puppy.

If you are overly domineering or physical (using your hands to chastise) when education, you could psychologically scar a puppy for life, regardless of its temperament.

The proper diet also plays a huge part in how well adjusted your puppy will be. Poor nutrition can be just as detrimental as poor or insufficient guidance.

You are Your Puppy's Educator

If you choose to have a puppy, you must take full responsibility for your pup's welfare, education, and entertainment.

It helps to remember that if the puppy had remained within its canine family, with its siblings and mother to watch over it, it would have received much-needed education and interaction from them in a canine way.

Many people mistakenly believe that puppies do not need any education and that they should just fall into place and be naturally well behaved. Even humans do not possess this much natural ability or intelligence, and we are far more intellectually advanced than canines.

Just as children and guidance with toilet training and social skills, so do dogs.

Owning a puppy is a huge responsibility for you to take on, but there is someone who can lighten the burden for you.

The Bark Busters Promise

Bark Busters therapists are trained to offer all the advice you need for rearing and education a trouble-free puppy. We offer information on toilet training, social skills and socialisation, education and behavioural control in and around other family members.

Our goal is to assist you and your puppy to live in harmony and to provide you with a clearer understanding of your puppy's needs, how a dog's mind works and what makes it tick.

If you are considering a puppy, Bark Busters can offer advice on selecting the right breed for your needs and the right sex to match perfectly without animals in your household.

We have information about early puppy education, advanced group obedience and in-home services. We can advise you as to which is the best choice for you and your puppy.

You can contact the Bark Busters therapist nearest you by phoning the toll-free number listed on the back of this book.

Identifying Your Puppy's Personality

Knowing the personality of the puppy you have or the one you are going to select is important when it comes to its education.

All puppies are individuals, so education techniques have to be tailored to the dog's personality and should not be a one-size-fits-all approach.

Bark Busters therapists are carefully trained to recognize the differences in temperament types and to tailor a program to that particular puppy's personality and temperament.

If you have attended a Bark Busters puppy class or had a home visit, you already have had you puppy's personality and temperament checked and assessed.

Selecting the Proper Refocusing Level

Refocusing is our way of letting a dog or puppy know that it needs to focus on you. The goal is to get the dog's focus onto you instead of being focused on whatever else it sees or any mistake it is making.

In order to educate the puppy and guide it to the behaviour you want, it needs to be focused on you.

Like people, all dogs are different and have varying personalities and temperaments, so you will need to ensure that you do not overwhelm your puppy. Very timid, shy puppies will not require too much effort to get them refocusing, whereas more assertive pups might require a more determined effort to gain their focus.

How do you work out the level of refocusing that is right for your puppy?

The foolproof way is to adopt a sliding scale of refocusing. Begin with a very mild level and work your way up the scale until you get an appropriate response.

Because dogs naturally growl when disapproving of something, it naturally follows that a growl will work as 'a communicative tool' to get your puppy looking in your direction for guidance. Usually, a soft growl for the shy, timid types and a stronger growl for the more determined puppies will work.

Determined
versus
shy

Chapter 4

The 'Thinking' Behind Bark Busters Training

When it comes to educating, there is virtual maze out there when new puppy owners are searching for assistance. Many people ask: *"which technique should I use when educating my puppy?"*

We are often asked what sets the Bark Busters method of early puppy education and dog training apart from the other methods.

We believe there are several aspects that distinguish us, but the most important one is the unique technique we use. It is kind, gently, nonphysical, dog friendly, and extremely quick and effective because it is based on the way canines naturally communicate.

Bark Busters is the world's premier dog training company and the world's largest professional dog training organisation of its kind.

We believe we have achieved this status because of our unique canine education methods. The service we provide to our clients is second to none.

Bark Busters methods are designed to encourage puppies and dogs to use their brain and to become a 'thinking dog'.

What is a Thinking Dog?

A 'thinking dog' is a dog that, once it has been shown something, can then work things out for itself, changing any undesirable behaviour to a desirable behaviour.

Case History

Clara was a well-bred German Shepherd puppy whose bad behaviour baffled her owners. Her owners had bred German Shepherds for 20 years and thought they had seen it all. They were bewildered when Clara, at a very young age, began to bark uncontrollable each time they tried to leave her alone. She was inconsolable and would squeal loudly when amy family member left the house.

After trying everything they knew, they called Bark Busters. We interviewed Clara's owners at length over the phone.

On arrive at the home, we expected to meet an absolutely, crazy, unresponsive dog. We were pleasantly surprized to find a dog that appeared clam and very responsive to us, with an outgoing, friendly nature. We knew instantly that this was not a bad dog, just a misguided one. We decided to view her behaviour before commencing any treatment.

We asked the owners to demonstrate what Clara would do when they left the house. Leaving her in the apartment, they closed the door and left. We waited with the owners quietly outside. Clara went into a frenzy, squealing and barking while she pawed and scratched at the door.

Once we had seen enough, we signaled for the owners to go back into the house. We began our therapy, which consisted of teaching the owners to be their dog's leaders in order to educate Clara about her role in the family and how to behave around the house.

Unbeknow to her owners, we could see that Clara had been running the household. She was rushing through doors ahead of the owners, pushing the owners with her body and sitting in their chairs. In Clara's eyes, her owners had no leadership status; she was treating them like subordinates. That was why she behaved so crazily when they left. *signs of dominance; mindful*

Clara responded to the therapy very quickly. She wanted to give up control, but had never been properly guided in the past.

This was all normal routine for us and we have seen results like this many times before. What made us smile was the amazement of her owners. Clara immediately stopped barking when the owners refocused her unwated behaviour into desired behaviour.

We decided to check out another problem. Whenver a family member went into the bedroom, Clara would go beserk. We were told that normally she would leap up and jump at the door, barking uncontrollable.

We set up a situation where one owner went into the bathroom and the other stayed with Clara to educate her, refocus her behaviour, and praise her when she co-operated.

This time, as Clara started to jump on the door, she appeared to be thinking about what she was doing and seemed to have second thoughts about what to do. She suddenly stopped, looked around at her owner, and stepped down.

Clara had become a 'thinking dog'.

How Does the Bark Busters Technique Work?

The Bark Busters techniques use the same system dogs use to communicate with each other and to establish leadership. It is therefore instantly recogniable by the dog and not something it has to learn. Dogs respond instantly in most cases.

Because dogs use guttural sounds and body language to communicate with each other, we believe that it is counterproductive to speak to a puppy in sentences or to use copious amounts of words.

The puppy has no comprehension of our language but can learn to comprehend the sound of spoken words and relate them to certain actions. While a puppy understands its own canine language instantly, it takes time for it to learn the human language, and in some cases it can take months.

The Bark Busters system, which uses 'canine communication' methods, takes minutes for the dog to learn. The longest part of a sessions is spent teaching the owners.

We actually communicate with the dog in its own language, unlike other techniques that are geared more to being only human-friendly rather than dog-friendly and dog focused, which use human-type language such as "no". — *focus on gutteral, animal languest. Best to emphasize*

A dog goes not naturally comprehend the word "no". It has to learn it and this, again, slows the learning process. We believe that it is never as effective as the growl, which the dog instinctively understands.

In much the same way that Monty Roberts, aka the 'The Horse Whisperer', has gradually changed things in the horse world, many dog owners are now following the teachings of Bark Busters. They have realized that the word "no" is not as effective as the growled "bah" word and are changing their way of addressing undesirable behaviour in their dogs.

When Bark Busters began in the early 80's, absolutely no one other than our organisation used the "growl technique". Bark Busters has spread to other parts of the world, and we are making an impact in many countries.

Bark Busters therapists do use communication commands and instructional words in training – however superfluous – but they are used in connection with the "bah" and body language rather than in place of the guttural sounds and body language that the dog naturally comprehends.

This is not to say that we cannot use words to communicate with our puppies, we can. Nonetheless, if we have the way and means of communicating using 'canine language' and know that it is faster than human language, why not use that form of communication?

Motivational Communication Therapy

At Bark Busters, we use what we call "motivational communication therapy", as well as communicating with the dog in its own language. This technique is used to get the dog to change its focus onto the owner rather than on what it is doing. This gives the owner the opportunity to motivate the dog using the dog's language before praising it for ceasing the bad behaviour.

This type of training actually turns the dog into a 'thinking dog'. Now, when it is about to misbehave, it remembers the distraction that occurred previously and will stop what it was about to do to instead of seeking out the praise as its reward.

→ such as

Chapter 5

Steps to Having a Well-Behaved Puppy

Communication

As previously mentioned here in order to ensure accurate communication with our puppies, it is vitally important that we copy their language as closely as possible by using both guttural sounds and enticing body language.

It makes sense to communicate in the dog's language because it means we are not slowing the learning process by having them to first learn our language. Similarly, it would be difficult for you to comprehend this book if we were written in a foreign language. You would first have to get over the hurdle of understanding the language.

I guess we could say the dog's first language is 'dog language' and its second language is human language. Therefore, it makes good sense to communicate with your puppy in its first language if you want quick results.

Body Language Communication

Dogs rely heavily on body language to communicate their every thought. If they are feeling frightened, weak, or showing respect, they will lower their height. If they are feeling confident and strong, they will increase their height and stand as tall as possible.

Other dogs read these signs quickly and act accordingly. Therefore, it follows that if you want to display the signs of leadership, you need to display the proper body language, that which the dog would associate with a dog that has leadership qualities.

You must stand as tall and as straight as you can. If you are sitting or lying down and trying to get your pup to behave, your body language is a contradiction and tells the pup that you are weak and a pushover. Even if you growl, it will make no difference because your puppy relies primarily on the messages relayed via your body language rather than what is being relayed via your growl.

The growl can be misinterpreted as 'fear' rather than superiority because your body language is expressing 'fear' or 'compliance'.

Example: When you stand tall and totally still, you emulate he actions of an assertive, confident dog.

Verbal Communication

Puppies, like children, need direction and education. To develop normally, they need rules and guidelines as to what is acceptable and unacceptable behaviour.

Like children, a puppy will go about doing what it feels like doing until you direct its energies and focus onto more positive things. This is how it learns. It has no concept of right or wrong; this it learns from you by experiencing a great rewarding experience (praise and encouragement) when it focuses its attention on something we would prefer it to focus on.

An example would be if a two-year-old child was walking around kicking people. Imagine if, despite their disapproval of the behaviour, the child's parents took no action. Their silence would send the message to the child that this behaviour is acceptable.

Some puppy owners become frustrated and annoyed when their puppy misbehaves, and yet they give it no direction or education. They may punish their puppy for the undesirable behaviour, but generally the punishment is administered after the fact, in some cases it is also a physical reprimand which is totally unnecessary and unfair and only serves to create 'fear'.

This leads the puppy to feelings of insecurity and can create a situation where the puppy has no confidence in its mixed canine, human family. It begins to display exaggerated submissive signs and experiences a strong sense of fear every time the owner approaches. It might even urinate.

Additionally, the owner could begin to dislike the puppy. It can appear to the owner that the pup is stupid or stubborn. If this situation is allowed to progress, the owner might soon be looking for a new home for their puppy.

Owners less willing to find it a new home might condemn the puppy to a situation where no one in the family interacts with it, or where it is confined indefinitely to a pen or crate.

To develop an understanding of its learning capabilities and communication skills. As already stated, puppies and dogs communicate via body language and guttural sounds.

If you choose to use only human language with your puppy, you could equate it to you taking a course in a foreign language. You would understand it eventually, but your learning would be severely hampered by first having to learn the language.

It is important that you communicate your directions to your puppy in the right way. Dogs cannot analyze, so your message of direction must be understood clearly and delivered at the right time.

Canines do not have the ability to reason; they do not possess the mental capacity that humans do. A human brain is made up of three sections: the cortex (our subconscious), the intellect and the reasoning. Canines have only two: the cortex and the intellect.

The most effective way to communicate your displeasure to a puppy or dog is exactly the same way that dogs would voice their disapproval with each other: that is, with a growl.

This will remove all doubt: your puppy will know instantly what you are saying.

The growl must be uttered in the same way the puppy's mother would growl. This should be coupled with the appropriate body language, and you must see recognition (compliance signs and focus) from your puppy.

If your puppy does not react, then either the sound is not right, or your puppy does not have enough respect for you. How you can achieve more respect from your puppy is covered in Chapter 6.

Learning to Speak 'Dog'

The word we use at Bark Busters is *"bah"*.

"Bah" is not a magic word on its own. Spoken in a normal tone, it would probably be ignored by your puppy. It must be vocalized in the same way a dog would growl, with a deep guttural tone.

If you have a puppy that is ignoring your growl, rest assured that you are failing in other areas of your role; the pup does not acknowledge you as its leader.

If this is the case, you should seek professional assistance by speaking with your local Bark Busters therapist.

To get your message across, you must catch the puppy in the act or when it is indicating that it is about to commit the crime, not after the fact.

Scene Setting — Proactive "Set the scene"

Scene setting simply means setting up a situation where you know your puppy will misbehave and then being ready to address its mistakes as soon as they occur.

Scene setting allows you to relay the message to your puppy in a proactive manner, instead of a reactive one in which the puppy has already gotten away with the bad behaviour while you are still trying to take action.

The benefit of scene setting is that you can teach your puppy very quickly, rather than over a period of time, because you create those situations in which your puppy misbehaves, then immediately address the behaviour by refocusing the puppy.

For example, think of all the situations in which your puppy misbehaves. Your puppy may misbehave when you get out of bed, jumping and barking at your feet. When you try to make breakfast, it tugs at your night gown. Since you are in a hurry to get ready for work, you don't have the time to spend on education.

You rush off to shower and the puppy stands outside the door barking and scratching. Then, when your friends visit, your puppy barks at the door and jumps all over them as they try to enter the house. As you and your friends leave the house, the pup begins to bark.

In reality, this could take two hours to happen, but if you set up these scenarios, you could deal with hem in less than half an hour. Instead of waiting for all of these things to happen, set them up. Have your friend come by another day when you will have the time to address the behaviour, rather than when you are rushing to go somewhere.

Once you have taught your puppy that you do not approve of this behaviour, you will not have to take much time to address the behaviour when you are busy, rushing to go out or cooking a meal. If executed correctly, a 'one-time' refocusing exercise will probably do the trick.

Refocusing Your Puppy

Now that you understand the type of body and voice communication you need, the exact timing required, and the importance of scene setting, you can begin your puppy's education.

To ensure that you are in a position of strength when dealing with any bad behaviour, you must remember that your puppy does not understand your language. Keep to guttural sounds already mentioned. Do not become physical, and use refocusing with your puppy using only the Bark Busters guidelines.

Warning: A puppy that is overly compliant or groveling is responding to its owner's body language. The owner is angry inside and cannot hide it. The puppy reads this and reacts accordingly. Dogs possess an uncanny ability to detect their owners' anger, regardless of how well the owners might try to hide it.

Understanding Signs of Co-operation and Compliance

We now have established that physical compliance signs by the puppy are very good signs, provided they coincide with refocusing the dog while it is in the act of doing something wrong.

If, on the other hand, the compliant body language coincides with play, normal activities, or your arrival home, then it means you are being too assertive and should soften the refocusing and administer more praise. It may also indicate that previously you might have used physical means (picking up or dragging back to the scene of the crime) and you need to learn to communicate vocally.

When to Praise

Praise and encouragement are just as important as the refocusing of your puppy away from bad behaviour. The praise lets your puppy know that you are pleased with its choice and that it has responded favourably to your direction.

Be sure to use the proper voice tone when praising. See *The Proper Voice Tone* in the following section.

Praise should closely follow your puppy's decision to co-operate and when it has stopped the bad behaviour but never during the undesirable behaviour and must be delivered in an inviting, light tone of voice, coupled with the right body language. Again, you should see the appropriate body language from your puppy (tail wagging, body relaxed, and mouth open).

Rules of the game

You could liken the proper tone for praise to the same tone people use when talking to babies.

The Proper Voice Tones

A common problem with many puppy and dog owners is that they use the wrong voice tones when attempting to communicate with their puppy or dog.

A harsh voice to a dog is the same as a growl. A high-pitched voice or sound is the same as the excited squeals puppies and dogs make when they greet each other.

½ tone

Voice Tones

Low-growl tone: Bah! For refocusing puppy's mistakes.

High-pitched tone: Good dog! When you see co-operation and compliance. Come! For praise and to call your puppy.

Normal-speaking voice: Sit, Stay, or Drop when you give commands.

The Proper Body Language

In situations where you lose control of an excited puppy, you must stand your ground. Never move towards the puppy or move about.

Example:

When calling your runaway puppy, stop in your tracks. Crouch and call your puppy to you in an inviting, pleasing voice. Stand up to your full height when your pup approaches.

Never chase it; you must stand your ground, or you can try to run in the opposite direction, to show the pup that you are the leader.

When addressing your puppy's mistakes, stand to your full height and use a deep guttural tone for refocusing.

Call your puppy to you for a pat; never go to your puppy to pat it.

Do not pat a pup that has rolled over on its back, this can cause a puppy to playfully snap and bite at your hands; instead, back away, crouch down and call it to you. Praise it when it does.

Chapter 6

The Proper Way to Educate a Puppy

Hands Off

Don't ever pick up your puppy to control it. Instead, crouch down to call it to you, or refocus its behaviour verbally.

Don't smack, push, or poke your puppy with your hand or a rolled-up newspaper, or grab its muzzle. These are all physical, harsh methods and will only make your puppy want to bite your hands next time you try to touch it.

Don't drag your puppy back to the 'scene of the crime'. You must catch the pup in the fact to refocus, praise, and educate it.

Don't try to tackle a puppy that you cannot catch. Run the other way or crouch down and call it to you in a high-pitched voice.

Don't roll your puppy over to prove authority, don't try to hold it down or alpha roll it. Your body language and guttural sounds will relay this and are less traumatic.

Don't grab your puppy's collar, the scruff of its neck, or grip its muzzle to control or address its behaviour.

Any form of physical force is unnecessary and will lead to problems. When you use any of the above actions, you trigger the natural "fight or flight" response in a dog.

Case History

The owner of a seven-month-old German Shepherd puppy named Caesar called our office one evening very distressed about his pup's behaviour. It had ferociously attacked him without apparent provocation. He told us that most of the dog experts he had spoken to were advocating euthanasia for Caesar, but his memories of the good times with his puppy made him seek other opinions.

We asked him what had happened on the day of the attack.

He said that some dog expert had told him to Alpha Roll his dog when he was a young pup. He said this appeared to work fine when his dog was a small puppy, but it became increasingly difficult to get him to submit as he grew.

Around about this time, another problem arose: Caesar had begun to bark at guests when they were visiting his home. The owner tried everything, but his dog only got worse.

The owner had discussed this problem with the previous trainer, who told him to try the Alpha Rolling technique again. He followed their instructions and would try to Alpha Roll his dog and wrestle it to the ground when it became aggressive at the front door.

He did this several times until one day when visitors arrived and he went to the front door, his dog attacked him suddenly from behind.

Now, why would a dog that has never bitten anyone suddenly attack its owner?

We believe the dog had begun to associate the knocking on the door with the impending punishment and he was unleashing a sneak attack while the owner was not looking.

We cannot stress enough, don't 'Alpha Roll' your dog!

Fight or Flight

Any use of physical force creates 'fight or flight' in the puppy. This simply means that if an owner has grabbed a puppy to drag it back to the scene of the crime, 'alpha rolled' it, or smacked it after he refused to come, it will create fear in the puppy. The fear will then create a flight response.

However, if the pup is being restrained by the collar, rolled over, held down, or being picked up, it cannot flee. Its only other option might be to fight. It learns quickly that if its owner grabs it, the quickest way to get him to let go is to bite his hand.

The Stop Signal

The most important and necessary tool in your box of verbal tools should be a word that tells your puppy you want it to 'stop' what it is doing immediately and focus on you.

How to Introduce the Stop Signal

Conduct this exercise in a small area using a toy or a ball as a distraction. Ask a family member or friend to help.

Begin by standing in one spot. Wait for your puppy to wonder off, then use the "bah" word which your puppy should respond to, to stop it in its trace, and encourage it to return to you.

The idea is to get your puppy to stay with you or to return to you immediately. Once your puppy is staying with you without moving away, you can introduce a greater distraction by having your assistant drop the chosen toy on the floor. The moment your puppy begins to walk toward the item use your refocus word "bah". Then the instant your puppy stops and returns, praise it lavishly. Once your puppy is reliable, introduce other distractions such as family members or friends.

The Proper Voice Tones

The sound you use when communicating with your dog is important. There is no need to yell at your puppy; dogs have excellent hearing. If educated properly from an early age, your puppy can be taught to respond to a soft, audible growl, but this takes patience and practice. The only time you may have to use a louder audible sound is during emergency situations; when a dog is attacking; or in a life-or-death situation.

The Clap Technique

The clap technique is designed to add emphasis to the growl and to amplify the impact. Loudly clap your hands once as you simultaneously "bah" at your puppy. Your goal is to have your puppy respond to your verbal direction alone.

Most puppies respond to the clap technique because it emulates the way another dog would snap, which they instinctively respect and comprehend.

The Water Squirter

How frequent?

Using a water squirter as emphasis has its limitations and is not one of our favorites, but it is helpful in some situations. You can use it to squirt the puppy at the precise moment it is misbehaving and at the same time growl "bah". Eventually the only thing required will be the sound of the growled word.

The problem with this technique is that it is visual and not always readily available, unlike the clapping technique that you can make appear and disappear at will and is always available.

This method can lead to situations where your puppy will ignore your requests when it does not see the squirter in your hand. Keep the squirter hidden behind your back until you use it. Note, however, that some clever pups see the hand behind the back as a subliminal signal. This is not vindictiveness on the puppy's part, it is just 'association'.

Your puppy has learned that it cannot jump on you or bite your fingers when you have this object, but it can when you don't.

Summing Up

Once you have developed your 'stop signal', use it for those times when you want to stop your puppy from doing something. In time you will be able to get your puppy to immediately respond to you no matter the situation.

Chapter 7

Toilet Training

The most common question we are asked by puppy owners is: "How do I toilet train my puppy?" Toilet training is easy if you have all the facts.

Basically, puppies are no different from children when it comes to toilet training. If you took a diaper off a baby, he would go to the toilet anywhere he pleased. Babies have no control over their bladder or bowel movements until they reach at least one year old.

Having said that. I have met some very diligent mothers who have toilet trained their babies from 14 months of age and other mums who have not had success until their child reached 3 years of age.

In each instance, it hinged on the parent's perseverance and diligence.

Puppies also have no control over their bladder or bowels. With regular toilet training, however, the development of good toilet habits will begin. Puppies learn faster than babies.

You must never punish a puppy for relieving itself in the house or in the wrong area. Gently pick it up to interrupt it, take it to the place where you have established a toilet area for the puppy and wait with it. You will want to wait because picking it up will make it forget what it was doing, and it may very well run out of the room with you and relieve itself in another area of the home.

When teaching your dog where it should go to the toilet, you must develop good habits from the outset. It is unreasonable to expect a puppy that was allowed to go to the toilet anywhere it pleased when it was young, to develop the right habits when it is older.

Dogs, like people, are creatures of habit. If our parents taught us to go to the toilet anywhere we liked, that is where we would go.

The best policy is to establish a designated toilet area for your puppy. Setting up a caged area which has a toilet pad or toilet box where you can leave your puppy to toilet, is the easiest way to teach a puppy to go to the toilet in the right place. If you allow your puppy to go to the toilet on the floorboards or carpet, it will then always go to the toilet on the floorboards or carpet. Its smell will be very strong in that area, so it will now consider that to be the toilet area.

Toilet Habits of Male vs Female Puppies

There are definite persistent differences between the sexes when it comes to toilet training. Male puppies and dogs usually urinate and defecate fairly quickly once they have found the right ground scent.

Females, on the other hand, will take that little bit longer, which becomes more apparent as they mature. You might wait ages for a female to find the right spot, while a male dog will go straight to the nearest tree or bush.

Selecting the Right Toilet Area

The toilet area must be established very early on when you bring your new puppy home. A penned area is important for busy people who don't always have time to stand and wait for a puppy to go to the toilet. It can also double as a playpen for your puppy when you need some well-earned breaks.

Some puppies might not want to go outside to the toilet if it is raining, snowing, or very windy. They also might not go if there is loud machinery nearby, or if the neighbour's dog is barking at them. Some timid dogs will run straight back in the house, forgetting why they were out there in the first place.

A pen that is erected on a grassed area is invaluable in these cases because this will help the pup face its fear. Ensure adequate shelter is provided.

Alternatively, place a leash on a puppy that is showing signs of fear and stay outside with it until it calms down.

You cannot expect a puppy to go outside on its own while scary things are happening, especially if the pack leader does not seem willing to accompany it.

Bah

If your puppy tries to run away, growl "Bah", and encourage it to come to you. Make sure you refocus all fear-related actions and encourage your puppy to follow you, praising your puppy when it does.

Likewise, an indoor toilet area that is near a running washing machine might also worry a timid pup and prevent it from wanting to enter the room where its toilet has been created, so give some thought to where you place the dog's toilet area.

Times Your Puppy Will Want to go to the Toilet

If you want your puppy to develop good toilet habits, you need to be aware that there are definite times when your puppy wants to relieve itself. They are as follows:

- Immediately after eating or drinking;
- After waking up from a sleep;
- After exuberant play;
- When frightened;
- After being in its crate for some time;
- When you arrive home and allow your puppy into the house.

You must learn to practice good management skills if you want your puppy toilet trained properly.

Block off all interior doors of your house. When you do, let the pup walk around inside, and make sure you watch it.

When you cannot watch over your puppy, place it in a playpen that contains a toilet pad or contains a little box lined with sand or grass.

You must never blame and punish a puppy that makes a mistake. It is your responsibility to be diligent, and a lapse of concentration on your part could result in the puppy going to the toilet in the house.

Like any baby, your puppy needs your patience and understanding during toilet training.

Recommended Cleaning Techniques

Use only gentle cleaning products when cleaning up after your puppy's accidents. Ammonia-based products can cause serious mental and physical problems to your puppy if inhaled. It is especially dangerous in a pen where a dog or puppy inhales the ammonia-based product over a period of time.

Furthermore, ammonia-based products will attract your puppy back to the spot you have just cleaned because these cleaners contain some of the same basic chemical components found in canine urine.

Cleaning Up Urine Accidents

Blot the stain, place a mound of paper towels directly onto the stain and lay a large weight or stack of books on top of the paper towels so that the moisture can be absorbed for half an hour.

Remove the paper towels and spray the soiled area with an odour neutralizer to camouflage the smell.

This paper technique is very effective if the mishap is caught early.

It generally removes almost all urine stains.

Due diligence is then required to ensure that the spot is not soiled again by the puppy. A tablespoon of vinegar in warm water if effective in removing the odour and will not encourage the puppy back to the spot.

Or use a sprinkle – or absorber-type product available from your Bark Busters therapist of a pet store. There are some products that soak up many times their weight and generally leave no stain or odour. Keep these products on hand at all times.

A product called Supa Sorb is very effective; we used it to clean Coca Cola off a white rug with, amazingly, no stain whatsoever. Speak to your local Bark Busters representative for more details.

Cleaning Up Droppings from Carpet or Rugs

Remove the feces using toilet paper and dispose.

Use a reliable dry carpet shampoo or stain remover and clean according to directions.

The quicker the stain is cleaned up, the better. Stains left for any length of time will usually remain because the puppy's feces and urine contain enzymes that stain the carpet permanently if left for too long.

How easily the droppings can be removed from the carpet depends largely on the quality of food you feed your puppy.

Inside Housed Puppies

Good management is vitally important here. All interior doors to carpeted areas must be closed off. Pups will always gravitate to carpeted areas when going to the toilet because these surfaces hold the strongest smell.

A puppy that cannot be watched at all times or is near areas that cannot be blocked off should be placed in its playpen.

Portable Dens / Doggy Crates

Puppies instinctively are reluctant to foul the area in which they sleep. Therefore, an effective method to house-train your puppy is to have it sleep in a crate.

Make sure that the crate is only large enough for the pup to stand up and turn around. Any larger, and you will be encouraging the puppy to go to the toilet in a corner where it does not sleep.

Do not leave your puppy in the crate for long periods without ample opportunity to relieve itself. Otherwise, it will be encouraging the puppy to go to the toilet in a corner where it does not sleep.

Dogs grow to love their dens / crates very much. Our dogs put themselves to bed at night in their respective crates.

Outside Housed Puppies

Even puppies that are housed outside could experience toilet problems. A puppy that is housed in a garage or on a verandah will not know that the grass is meant to be its area for toileting unless properly educated.

Section off an area that your puppy can call its own or erect a playpen on a grassy spot that you have selected to be your puppy's designated toilet area. This will establish good toilet habits from the beginning. Your puppy will learn that grass is where it should toilet. Sound educational and early basic training will also reduce the amount of destruction the pup will cause when left unattended.

A sandpit makes a great entertainment area because it can dig to find the cool on a warm day and the warmth on a cold day.

Check that all dangerous and precious items are picked up and put out of harm's way. Ensure that your puppy has ample shelter from the elements and plenty of fresh drinking water at all times.

Chapter 8

Early Basic Education

Teaching Your Puppy Not to Jump Up

Jumping up is one of the most common problems we work with at Bark Busters and yet it is one of the easiest to solve. We find that many puppy owners try to solve this problem the wrong way, often because they are looking at it from a human perspective.

Dogs need to be refocused at the precise moment they are doing the wrong thing.

When confronted with a dog that jumps up, people naturally recoil and react by pushing the dog away or stepping back. Nature has taught us that this defensive reaction will save us from attack by people or falling objects.

Nature, however, has taught dogs that a quick movement or pushing action by their opponent means that they want to play and wrestle.

So, it is easy to see why this problem of jumping up is so difficult for most people to solve.

The most effective way to stop jumping up is to freeze your body movement the instant the dog lifts its feet off the ground. As your dog is about to land on you, clap your hands firmly and growl "Bah".

Clapping mimics the way a more assertive dog would snap at the pup. This action is respected by most puppies.

Remember to praise the puppy the instant it drops to the ground again.

Be prepared every time your puppy tries to jump on you. Repeat the process each time it begins to lift its feet off the ground. Have all adult members do likewise and you will soon find that jumping is a thing of the past.

A Puppy that Jumps on Children

Dogs and pups view young children as puppies that have no pack status. In other words, they generally will not respect them or accept authority from young children.

If children are encouraged to discipline a puppy for its bad behaviour, problems could occur when the puppy, growing at a faster rate than the child, reaches maturity. In the dog's eyes, the child will still have no authority, and the matured dog is now likely to discipline the child for his insolence.

It is for this reason that the adults in the household must do all of the puppy education and refocusing. The adults should set up situations where the puppy jumps on the children. Have the children run around and play. When the puppy starts to jump on a child, the adults should growl and clap their hands while instructing the child to freeze.

Under no circumstances should the child refocus the puppy for its actions. If the education is executed as explained, the puppy eventually will accept the child's reaction of freezing as a subliminal message that it's making a mistake by jumping.

An adult must supervize all play times with puppies and children. If you cannot be present to watch the puppy and child interact, put the puppy away or in its playpen.

Getting a Puppy to Come When Called

One of the most common problems dog owners face is getting their dog to come when called. This problem usually starts early, often in the absence of effective communication between dog and owner.

What generally happens is that owners allow their puppy too much freedom before they teach it to return to them when requested. The pup is allowed to roam off leash when outside and soon, it finds adventure. The new scents and unexplored areas are such a big attraction that no amount of persuasion by the owners will get it to respond.

The pup bounds away, and the owners chase it (instead of remaining where they are or running in the opposite direction). The puppy views their actions as approval because it appears to the puppy that the rest of the family is following it.

The pup thinks: *"This is great! All of us are now following the scent (or chasing the cat)."* The puppy cannot perceive it as misbehaving because the leader is joining in.

However hard it may be, you must not allow your puppy off the leash unless it is in an enclosed area, or until it learns to come to you when called.

Starting the "Come When Called" Exercise

Puppies are like children in that they are easily distracted. The first new scent puppies detect will have them scurrying off to investigate. Thus, you need to be animated and excited to get your puppy to focus on you instead of the new, more interesting surroundings.

Before letting your puppy off lead, find an enclosed area where it cannot escape. Allow your puppy to wander around and sniff. When you are ready, back away a few feet, crouch down and call your puppy. Make your voice high pitched and exciting, then crouch down and encourage your puppy to come to you.

Call your puppy's name and say, *"come"* or *"here"*. Stay crouched. Clap your hands quickly while softly saying *"pup, pup, pup"* in a high-pitched voice.

Hold your ground. The soft clapping is an inviting sound as opposed to the single firm clap. Do not move towards your puppy or chase after it. This will only set up a chase-or-follow sequence, which will make your puppy run the other way.

If you get no response at all, practice the recall exercise in a smaller enclosure or use a long leash.

When your puppy comes to you, pet it, and slowly return to your full height while petting it. If your puppy attempts to move away, growl "Bah!".

Again, lower your height and praise your puppy the instant it responds or looks in your direction.

Do not allow the pup to wander off until you are confident that it will happily stay beside you. Use only a verbal correction. Do not attempt to grab or hold on to your puppy. It must stay on its own free will and because you have displayed leadership qualities showing that you are its pack leader. When the exercise is completed, say *"Free"* or another suitable word.

Gentle Handling

The proper use of your hands while educating is vitally important. At no time should you inflict pain or cause fear to get your puppy to obey you. Make sure you do not grab or hold onto your puppy. Your hands must be used only for patting during off-leash work.

You must never grab your pup to keep it with you or to admonish it for not coming to you previously. Dogs cannot analyze, they learn by association. They relate to what was happening at the time they experienced the discomfort, associating the discomfort with you rather than with the misconduct.

It is pointless to scold your puppy for something it did previously or after it has left the scene and is returning to you. You will only confuse and frighten the pup. It cannot understand what message you are trying to deliver. Any time you handle your puppy, do so gently. Otherwise, it will learn to avoid your hands completely and you will experience problems with anything you try to do with it in the future.

Walking Correctly on Leash

Your puppy can learn to walk calmly by your side, and this can be an easy exercise to teach if you begin in the right way and in the puppy's own yard. The reason to start this exercise in the dog's yard is because it has already sniffed everything on its property; the unknown smells in the street would be too distracting.

Dogs are natural pullers, and most dogs and puppies will pull when first placed on a leash. Do not rush to keep up with the puppy. Slow down and take slow, deliberate steps.

Using a loose leash, flick and release the leash saying "Bah" as you do so. This will let your puppy know immediately that you do not approve of the way it is pulling. The leash must never be taut. If your puppy runs to the end of the leash, move your hand forward quickly, creating slack in the leash, and then quickly flick the leash back again. How?

Stop walking and wait for your puppy to stop pulling before moving off again.

Repeat this several times, walking slowly and deliberately, then stopping until your puppy gets the message.

If you are walking your puppy and it throws itself to the ground, refusing to go any further, do not pick it up. Instead, face your puppy and crouch down. Call the puppy to you using an encouraging voice.

The puppy will learn to walk correctly only if it is allowed to take the steps itself without any dragging. Do not venture too far until your puppy is walking perfectly. Remember, puppies under six months of age must not be over-exercised because it can cause skeletal damage.

Teaching the Sit / Stay

The sit exercise will be the easiest exercise you will teach your dog. It is best done on leash because you will then have all of the controls. Be patient. A puppy's mind is everywhere.

Have your puppy by your left side. Gently gather the leash in your right hand while your left-hand rests on our puppy's hips. Say *"sit"*. Do not push or grip this are harshly because that will tent to make a puppy want to jump away from your hand.

All exercises must be carried out in a calm and controlled fashion, with no pressure placed on the puppy.

Step in front of your puppy as you turn and face it. If your puppy moves, growl "Bah!" and gently place it back on its original spot. As soon as your puppy sits, remove your hand. If the puppy pops up again, gently replace your hand while saying "Bah!".

Once you get your puppy to stay in the sit position, wait a couple of seconds and then return to it. Wait another couple of seconds and the say *"free"*, praising your puppy as you do.

Repeat this exercise four times and then move on to the next exercise. It is not wise to overtire a puppy without exercise.

Wait for two seconds and then allow your puppy to move off the spot by saying *"free"*. Again, remember to praise your puppy.

Chapter 9

Solving Common Problems

Puppies can have a myriad of problems. Like children, they are still learning the rules. Their world is an exciting and novel place full of adventure.

Do not expect your puppy to know right from wrong, it must learn that from you. If the education is not progressing well, you need to rectify the problem using proper communication techniques while being fair and consistent in order to achieve a proper education with good results.

Preventing Destructive Behaviour

Prevention is better than the cure. Bad habits are learned and become entrenched. It is better to develop positive habits right from the start. How can you be sure to do that?

You are creating the environment in which your puppy lives. You can choose to fill it with temptation or productive, educational toys and play areas. The choice is yours.

Outdoors

Be proactive when it comes to the environment you provide for your puppy. Think about all of the temptations in your yard prior to letting your puppy out.

- Are children's toys scattered within reach?
- Is the laundry flapping in the breeze and accessible to the puppy?
- Is your outdoor furniture accessible?
- Are precious potted plants on the patio?
- Are there gaps in the fence through which an adventurous puppy could squeeze?
- Is the garden shed locked and secured?
- Are shoes out of the puppy's reach?

By inspecting the puppy's environment and thinking about the worst possible scenario, you can stave off heartache and expensive repairs.

Indoors

The inside of your house is full of precious items and no amount of education may prevent the destruction of some household items. Remove your cherished possessions or protect them by spraying them with a deterrent.

Protect your TV remote controls and cables, indoor plants, clothes, shoes and slippers, wooden furniture, and baseboards. A playpen for your puppy, or a separate room where special items can be stored is a must in this situation.

Puppy Playpens

Puppy playpens can be purchased from most pet suppliers. Additionally, playpens made for toddlers are also ideal for small puppies. If your puppy stays outdoors, you can construct a playpen by sectioning off a part of the yard.

You could also make a playpen by knocking a few stakes into the ground and covering them with strong weld mesh or a similar rigid wire that does not allow the puppy to push its way out or to dig under the wire.

Precast fences such as pool fences are also suitable and will not allow the dog to climb. Speak to the people at your local fence or pool shop. The selected fence must be rigid and firm as puppies can push or dig under loose, flimsy fencing.

Barking and Aggression

Well-adjusted and well-bred puppies rarely bark. The only time you should expect some barking is during the first few nights. If you have a yappy puppy that tends to bark a lot, you must stop this immediately.

Barking and/or aggression should be addressed the instant the puppy starts to bark or growl. Refocus with your vocally growled "Bah" and praise the instant your puppy responds.

Most puppies will respond to the eight-step scale of refocusing method in Chapter 3. However, if your puppy is barking at things out of fear, the basic refocusing might not work for you. The puppy's fear of the unknown will generally overcome the usual reaction to any level of refocusing you might try.

If this is the case, you need to call your local Bark Busters representative. Do not delay, because a puppy that barks may have aggression problems or be a budding nuisance barker. These issues are best dealt with at the puppy stage before habits become ingrained. You should also contact Bark Busters if you have an aggressive puppy that cannot be controlled.

Chewing

It is natural for puppies to chew, just the way it is natural for young children to chew. In the early days, remember to keep your precious items well out of the puppy's reach.

Additionally, a product called Bitter Apple is a good deterrent and is widely used by Bark Busters for persistent chewers.

Bitter Apple is safe and effective and is available from your Bark Busters therapist.

Puppies do need to chew, however, supplying your puppy with several safe, chewy items will assist in dramatically reducing problems. Puppy teething rings (available from most pet shops or online shopping) are also great for puppies that are teething.

Hand Biting

Hand biting can stem from someone in the family playing roughly with your puppy.

Young children and adolescents are the greatest offenders. They tend to want to rough up the puppy and will thrust their hands towards it, playing a game that incites biting. All games must be sensible ones. If you follow the rule that 'hands are for petting only', you will have fewer problems with hand biting. However, if you have a puppy that is biting your hands, implement the following steps.

Step One:

When the puppy appears ready to bite your hand, freeze your hand on the spot, growl "Bah" at the puppy and wait for its reaction. It should stop and look at you.

When it responds, praise it. Then try to pet the puppy. If it tries to bite your hand again, repeat the above process.

If it appears that you have a determined puppy that refuses to stop regardless of how much you growl, you might need to escalate to Step Two.

Step Two:

Fill a water squirter with water. Keep it hidden behind your back and pet your puppy. If it tries to bite your hand, freeze the action and using your other hand, squirt the puppy while growling "Bah".

Again, praise the puppy when it stops biting. Squirt and growl when it starts again. This will usually discourage the most determined puppy, but you must be consistent.

The reason for the growling coinciding with the squirt of water is to condition your puppy to respond to vocal refocusing alone. Remember to freeze the actions of the hand that is about to be bitten and to squirt with the other hand. Pulling back will only encourage the puppy to persist.

Jumping Up

Again, freeze your action. By freezing, you are mimicking the reaction of an assertive dog, and this is a good deterrent to some would-be jumpers. Some puppies, however, are very determined and will keep jumping even if you freeze, so additional steps must be taken.

You will need to use your water squirter again. Wait for your puppy to lift its feet off the ground as it is about to jump on you. Squirt the pup, growling "Bah", and praise the instant it has all four feet on the ground. Repeat the process until the puppy stops jumping up. You will eventually gain control by just freezing the action and growling "Bah".

Chapter 10

Children and Your Puppy

Avoiding Common Problems

Many people believe that all children should own a dog, and they will go out of their way to purchase a puppy especially for their child. We believe that this could be fraught with danger if the proper steps are not followed.

As a rule, children under 12 years of age cannot safely establish leadership over a dog. This means that the dog will view the children as having no authority in the human/dog family unit. In general, a dog will ignore commands from a young child.

Dogs view children as playthings. Some dogs become very excited when children arrive at the house because children run around and scream. Adults, on the other hand, walk calmly.

In a puppy's mind, children are just other puppies. They hold no authority and are not considered part of the family unit hierarchy. This lack of family status can place an unsupervised child in danger. If a child were to mimic an adult by trying to discipline the household dog or puppy, the puppy or dog might chastise the child for his insolence. The scolding might be a snap, or it could be an all-out attack, depending on the dog's temperament, the child's reaction, and how severe the misdemeanour might have been.

Many dogs lose their lives because parents are not aware of how a dog's mind works. The horror of a dog snapping at a child is more than most parents can bear, when the dog was merely chastising the child for taking liberties. The dog was meting out its innate form of justice and was correcting the child for overstepping the boundaries of the family unit hierarchy.

The whole process may seem vicious and barbaric, but we must remember that this is the way dogs discipline each other; this is the dog's law, the law according to the pack. A person hits with his hands; a dog hits with its mouth. Note too, that if you use physical methods to deal with your puppy's misbehaviour, your puppy could very well emulate this when dealing with a child.

Dogs can be taught to respect children, but even well-educated dog might revert to the ways of the pack if left unattended with a child.

Remember the golden rule: "Never allow a child to discipline any dog". Nor should you leave a child alone with any dog or puppy. Teach your child to respect all dogs in the family. Children should never be allowed to hit, hurt, or tease dogs.

A child that is permitted to roughhouse with a family dog might be reprimanded by the dog that has had enough of the rough treatment. Also, children visiting the house could be in danger of being bitten. The dog has the impression that children mean pain, and some dogs will try to avoid pain by getting in the first bite.

We are called upon often to help with situations where the family dog has begun to snap at the household and visiting children.

Our investigations nearly always reveal that a child's previous actions have caused a large part of the problem. Most of the problems between dogs and children are created because a child has been allowed to hit or hurt the dog. When the dog retaliates, the owners react with horror as in the following case history.

Case History

Clancy, an eighteen-month-old Siberian Husky, was the most adorable and gentle creature on Earth until he went to live with a family that had an energetic three-year-old boy.

Clancy was six months old when he was bought from a breeder as a pet for the boy. For many months he tolerated the child's rough advances. The boy would hit Clancy in his face and stand on Clancy's toes.

In the beginning, Clancy would see the boy coming and try to move away. He no doubt looked to his owners to intervene, but the boy was their only child, and, in their eyes, he could do no wrong. Clancy obviously realized that he was a plaything at the child's mercy. If the leaders were not going to deal with the problem, he would have to take action to protect himself.

The next time the child cornered him, Clancy snapped to warn him to back off. The child, however, was not in the habit of listening to anyone, let alone a mere dog, and just kept coming.

Clancy knew he would have to take more drastic steps to make the child stop his advances, so he leapt at the child's face and nipped him on the cheek.

Clancy had hit pay dirt this time, the child screamed and immediately back off, running to his mother. Clancy would have felt pretty happy with himself; he had taught the child a lesson and he felt sure the child would not bother him again.

He was right. The next day Clancy was put to sleep at the local animal welfare shelter.

These types of stores always sadden us, because no one was given the opportunity to speak on the dog's behalf. If we want to stop hearing stories like this, parents need to educate their children on how to behave around dogs.

Dally Says is a child safety video produced by Bark Busters to teach children how to behave around dogs and how to avoid being bitten. It can be purchased from your local Bark Busters therapist.

Creating Harmony with Puppy and Children

Not only are we responsible for the behaviour of our puppies and dogs and how they act around our children, but we are also responsible for the behaviour of our children around our puppies and dogs.

Children and dogs must be supervized at all times when together. No ifs and/or buts. Parents must teach their children to treat all animals with the utmost respect.

If an exuberant child cannot be controlled, the kindest thing you can do is find the puppy a new home where its rights will be respected by the whole family.

Responsibility for Rearing the Puppy

"He's your pet and you must look after him." We have lost count of how many times we have heard parents tell this to their children.

Children should not be given the huge responsibility of looking after a puppy without adult assistance and supervision.

By all means, children may participate in the care and grooming of their pets, but only under strict adult supervision. They must not be allowed to discipline a dog or puppy. It is here that adults must take full responsibility for a pet brought into the household; parents cannot morally wash their hands of the responsibility of their dog's education. Children should not have this responsibility placed on their young, inexperienced shoulders.

We are aware that the *"It's your pet; therefore, you must look after it"* theory stems from the belief of many parents that their children should be responsible for the pet they had asked their parents to buy. Unfortunately, this does not work in practice because the children lack the understanding of all that a pet requires.

Parents would not think of asking a child to be responsible for the rearing and caring for a new baby sister or brother. Yet, we continually see situations where children are expected to be responsible for a creature that is agile, difficult to understand, and can easily outsmart them.

Who Should Educate the Puppy?

Children do not possess the capability or authority it takes to educate a puppy or dog to teach it right from wrong.

There are many 'dog experts' who say that children should be encouraged to educate and be responsible for the family dog or puppy. We believe that this is a dangerous philosophy because few children or family situations are conducive to this practice. All family circumstances and dog/puppy temperaments must be assessed individually before such advice is given.

The adults in the family must ensure that the children's family status is established in the following way:

- The children always precede the dogs and puppies through doorways, up and down stairs, and when going from room to room.
- No dog or puppy is allowed to steal food from a child, or to be assertive to a child.
- The adults must be the only ones to address the behaviour of a puppy or dog that snaps at an approaching child.
- Only adults (or children over 12 years old) in the family can educate the puppy or dog.
- Children should never be left unattended with any dog or puppy.

- Children under 12 years of age must never be allowed to chastise the dog or puppy for bad behaviour.
- Adults should always monitor children's actions when around the puppy or dog.
- Children must be taught to respect all animals.

GREAT KIDS
Guidelines!

Chapter 11

Visitors and Your Puppy

Interactions between visitors and your puppy should be monitored. If this is going to be too difficult, bring the puppy out after the visitors have settled in. Put the puppy on a leash to meet your guests.

Do not allow any rough play or exuberant behaviour with the puppy on the part of the visitors. They may, however, offer your puppy a treat, which should be dropped on the ground. Walk the puppy on leash near the visitors to get its treat and then put the puppy away. This will create less excitement and anxiety towards visitors, and the puppy will have a lasting memory that visitors represent something pleasant, not something to be feared or to become too excited about.

We have found that many aggression problems in dogs stem from those times when visitors behaved in such a way that the dog now has traumatic memories of their rough or thoughtless treatment. Over-exuberance problems can arise when visitors play games that encourage the puppy to act silly each time people visit.

Some male guests will want to play hand games with your puppy, roughing it up. This only creates future handling problems because the puppy will believe that all hands are for biting each time a human hand comes near it. Discourage rough games between puppy and guests.

Prevention of Influenced Behaviour

As we have pointed out, most unwanted actions in *Wow.* puppies can be caused by a person using rough *"most"* treatment during play or discipline. The strict monitoring of play, activities, or attempts to address behaviour by visitors or family is vitally important in determining how well adjusted your puppy will be when it reaches adulthood.

Danger Signals

Again, puppies are like children when it comes to the way they test the boundaries. Puppies will do only what they are permitted to do.

The serious problems of ankle and hand biting are usually human taught. As a puppy playfully bites at the hands or ankles, the person reacts by pulling away. This sets up a chain reaction where the puppy persists, and the human keeps reacting; the puppy gets excited, and the practice continues.

Freezing the action, followed by a growled "Bah" will work on most puppies. This allows you to refocus the puppy verbally while it is in the act of biting. The stillness of the hands or ankles will act as a deterrent.

If this does not work, follow the procedure for refocusing mentioned in Chapter 5.

Benefits of Ongoing Education

To raise a well-behaved dog, you will need to spend time educating your puppy. The first six months are its formative months and the most important time of your puppy's life. What it learns now will remain with it forever. Postponing education until the pup is older will only make your job more difficult. Your puppy could suffer untold psychological problems if it does not receive the right grounding early in its life.

Schedule regular bonding and educational sessions with your puppy. Make the sessions short but productive, and refocus the unwanted behaviour as instructed while you praise your puppy each time it gets it right. Also remember you are your puppy's educator. There is no one else who will provide this education; it is your responsibility. Regular education is a must and will help you and your puppy achieve a strong bond. Dogs are lifelong learners and actually enjoy educational interactions that enhance the human and canine bond.

Chapter 12

Grooming Your Puppy

Do It Yourself Grooming the Stress-Free Way

We hear many stories of people being bitten by their puppy or dog when they were attempting to groom it. Among themselves, dogs will allow grooming only by more assertive dogs, so dog owners are generally bitten because the dog does not view them as having more status than they do, in the family hierarchy.

Before you try to groom your puppy, you must have already established yourself as having more authority than your puppy in other situations, as explained in Chapter 5.

To begin grooming, put a leash on your puppy. Place the puppy on a sturdy table and start brushing. If your puppy reacts, or if it tries to bite or play, freeze the actions of the hand holding the brush, growl "Bah" and flick the leash with your other hand, letting your puppy know you do not approve of its behaviour.

Once your puppy stands still and allows you to groom it without wiggling, stop brushing and praise it lavishly. Then, allow your puppy to go free.

Grooming time can be extended a little at each session. Continue in this fashion for a couple of weeks, adding a little extra time each day until your puppy begins to look forward to being groomed.

You can also examine your puppy. Look in its ears and mouth, and pick up its paws, refocusing any undesirable behaviour as you go. You will be preparing your puppy for veterinary examinations.

Scheduling the Right Grooming Parlour

It is important to always have a well-groomed puppy. Short-coated puppies of course are easier to groom than long-coated ones. Some long-coated puppies, regardless of how diligent you are with their grooming, will have to visit a grooming parlour for clipping and coat stripping at some time in their lives.

It is important to your puppy's well-being that you check out the grooming parlour before leaving it there to be groomed. Ensure that the members of the grooming staff have competent dog skills; they must be patient with puppies and implement no harsh disciplinary action while on their charges.

Once you have selected a grooming parlour, make sure you will be allowed to stay with your puppy while it is being groomed. You will need to show them the best way to get your puppy to behave and accept the grooming.

If you have practiced brushing and grooming your puppy from an early age, you should have no problems showing the groomer how well behaved your puppy can be if handled correctly.

Bark Busters provide a service where they can assist an owner whose dog or puppy has a specific grooming problem.

Chapter 13

Socializing Your Puppy

There is much discussion today about how important it is to socialize a puppy. We firmly believe that dogs and puppies need to be exposed to family dogs and possible selected gentle dogs. They do not need to play or interact with other dogs outside their immediate family but should be tolerant of them.

Puppies need to be exposed to other dogs, traffic noises, children playing, dogs barking, livestock running around, as well as the loud noises of lawn mowers, weed eaters, and vacuum cleaners. Your puppy must learn to tolerate these everyday noises and events without chasing or barking at them.

On leash control in these situations is a must. Walk your puppy on a leash near as many of these distractions as possible and refocus your puppy every time it reacts negatively to a situation. Your puppy needs to learn how you, the leader, behave around these situations and that it needs not be fearful. If you remain cool and confident as you calmly refocus your puppy's negative responses, your puppy will not be frightened by these noises and circumstances.

If you attempt to socialize your puppy and discover that it becomes agitated to the degree that you cannot control its actions, contact your local Bark Busters therapist for assistance.

Dealing with an Antisocial Puppy

If you have an antisocial puppy that is becoming aggressive when it meets other dogs, you will want to understand how your dog's pack hierarchy instinct (the pecking order) plays a role in your dog's antisocial actions.

Most antisocial problems occur at the puppy level when owners are trying to get their puppy to be friendly with other dogs. People find it very entertaining to allow their dogs to romp and play. The problem with this scenario, however, is that dogs do not play with other dogs for the sheer fun of it, they actually use these games as a test of superiority. You could compare this to army maneuvers; the army conducts maneuvers to prepare for war and test how its soldiers will perform in battle, not as a form of entertainment.

When dogs play, each dog is determining the strength and capabilities of the other dog to see which will be the most assertive and have more authority.

Therefore, insisting that your dog be friendly, and play is not wise and can place unnecessary pressure on a puppy with an antisocial personality. You can liken it to people who don't feel comfortable in the company of strangers; they prefer to sit alone at parties and would really prefer not to be there.

Antisocial problems stem from the way your dog relates to other dogs. They are based on the puppy's personality and natural instinct and, quite possibly, what happened when it was first introduced to other dogs. When a dog meets another dog for the first time, the other dog may incite fear if it tries to assert authority over the inexperienced adolescent dog. That fear can turn to aggression the next time the inexperienced dog is put in the same situation.

The dog has now learned from experience that when it meets dogs in the park, in the street, or at the playground, it has one of two choices: to be assertive, or to be overwhelmed and frightened.

To the untrained eye, these challenges from other dogs can look like playful moves, but to a frightened, antisocial dog or puppy, they speak volumes.

A dog that stares at another dog, turns its head a certain way, or holds its tail in a certain way, could be saying to the antisocial dog: *"I'm the boss. You have no status."* This could then motivate the frightened dog to attack first in an effort to avoid being bullied.

Dogs that are bullied by partner dogs can also have aggression problems. Dogs stare when threatened: a confident dog can control its mate simply by staring. Owners would not necessarily pick up on this subtle sign. The result is generally that one dog could attack the other. Humans are also at risk of being attacked by a dog that is regularly bullied in this fashion, especially if they stare at the dog.

Dealing with Aggression to Other Dogs

You must first understand that it is not necessary for your dog to fraternize with dogs it meets on a walk. In the wild, dogs are never friendly with neighbouring dogs because they are protective of their own territory and food, and this protectiveness is still instinctive in some dogs.

When re-educating an aggressive puppy, let it know you are a strong leader who will protect it. You are the one who makes all decisions for the family. With firmness and consistency, make it clear to the pup that you will not tolerate any aggression.

Let your dog know by example that you will not subject it to a situation where it feels threatened. You can achieve this by taking it to several safe areas free of marauding dogs.

Chapter 14

Pack Mentality vs Socialisation

When it comes to socialising with other dogs, we at Bark Busters have a difference of opinion with the general mainstream thinking in the dog world. Many people in today's society extol the importance of socialising your puppy with other puppies. They believe this will stave off aggressive tendencies.

We believe that puppies have to know and tolerate other puppies and dogs, but we do not believe that they should play with other dogs outside their immediate family unit.

Our reasoning here is that dogs are instinctively pack animals. They will naturally form into packs, which can consist of human and dog packs, or all dog packs. These packs then generally remain constant. Canine rules and pecking orders are established, creating stability, confidence, and a feeling of security in the dog.

As previously mentioned, when puppies and dogs engage in what we refer to as 'play', they are actually carrying out the equivalent of army maneuvers. 'Play' to a dog is our equivalent of 'war games'. It's their way of testing their opponent's strength. Who will be in charge? Who will not?

Puppies that react violently to dogs outside their immediate pack are generally viewed by society as social misfits, and other dog owners try to avoid them.

They are, however, the victims of the new off leash areas that can sometimes create more problems than they solve. Problem altercations generally occur near the entrance where newcomers enter the park, and the established groups let them know who is in charge.

Don't get us wrong, we believe off leash areas are a great way of exercising your dogs, providing you have full control and providing your puppy is fully immunized. Nevertheless, they are best visited when there are no other dogs around and you are able to allow your puppy or dog to romp, sniff, and run around without fear of persecution.

We believe that off leash areas are more for the benefit of the dog owners than they are for the dog. It is a way for people who own dogs to get together and chat about their puppies and dogs. Although there is no harm in this, problems arise when a puppy or dog cannot cope with the park because of the reasons mentioned here.

Although most dogs and puppies are fine with socialisation at off-leash parks, many cannot cope because of the dog's natural laws, leaving them to look like social misfits and their owners to feel like bad parents. All of these antisocial problems could be avoided if puppy and dog owners are aware of how to socialize their pets correctly.

If you want to know more about the Bark Busters way of educating puppies, speak to your local therapist who can elaborate on home puppy lessons and Bark Busters puppy schools (available in selected areas).

Avoiding Dangerous Situations

In a perfect world where all owners knew the correct way to socialize a puppy, there would be no problems when you were out walking with your puppy. Unfortunately, people don't know the problems that they can encounter or instigate by allowing their dogs and puppies to run up to every dog they see in an effort to make friends.

We have seen many situations where unsuspecting puppy owners have allowed their new puppy to meet and greet other dogs in the street or at the beach with disastrous results. Often such altercations result in the little puppy being attacked and spending time in surgery being stitched up.

What usually happens is that the puppy sees a dog, runs off to greet it, and jumps all over it. The other dog might view this as a breach of proper canine protocol and could reprimand the puppy for its insolence. This is normal canine behaviour.

The result is much the same as it would be at the off-leash area. The pup learns early on that there are only two rules in life – to bully or be bullied.

Case History

The story of a Great Dane named Samson brings home how the wrong type of socialisation can create tragic victims. Samson was the recipient of just such abuse when he was a little puppy.

Samson was a normal, little fun-loving puppy until one day at the park. In his innocence, he ran up to a full-grown dog. The dog reprimanded him for his impertinence and attacked him. From that day, Samson's personality changed. He became fearful of other dogs and would snap and growl at them if they came within reach of him, fearing a similar attack would occur.

His owner became distressed. As Samson gained strength and height, he tried to keep Samson away from other dogs as much as he could. He began taking Samson to the park in the early hours of the morning and in the evenings when there were no other dogs around.

This worked well until the day a man and his Chihuahua walked into the park. The man slipped the leash off his little charge, and it bounded towards Samson and his owner. Samson immediately ran to hide behind his owner. It looked ridiculous: here was this giant dog hiding from a tiny Chihuahua.

Samson's owner yelled a warning to the Chihuahua's owner to get hold of his dog. The man laughed, *"he's only a Chihuahua"*, the man called back. *"He won't hurt him."* But before Samson's owner could comment further, Samson sprang from behind him and pounced on the Chihuahua, whose owner screamed in horror.

The little dog's body now lay limp on the ground and Samson was back behind his owner shivering. The man picked up his little dog and ran from the park no doubt toward the nearest vet.

These tragic events could have been avoided if, as a puppy, Samson had been socialized properly by his owner and not allowed free reign in the first place.

The victim's misfortune could also have been avoided if the Chihuahua's owner had not assumed that all dogs are friendly.

The Correct Way to Socialize Your Puppy

In light of the case history above, you must be wondering how you should socialize your puppy in a way that will not create future problems.

The best way to socialize a puppy with other puppies is on a leash and under your supervision. A puppy must learn to tolerate other dogs and puppies, but it is not absolutely necessary for it to fraternize or play with them. They may be allowed to sniff other puppies but not allowed to bully or be bullied. No puppy should be introduced to adult dogs, as some adult dogs might snap or attack puppies for no reason.

Puppies must be kept away from adult dogs and should never be allowed to romp with, or jump on, other puppies.

It is for this reason that we suggest you visit off-leash areas only when there are no dogs around or after your puppy reaches 12 months of age. You should confine the socialisation of your puppy to those times when you meet dogs and puppies during your normal everyday walks and only when both dogs are on leash.

Visiting a leash-free park during peak times with an antisocial dog on leash is not a good idea. Other dogs that are off leash could still approach your puppy. In this situation, your dog will become even more frantic or aggressive because, since it cannot move away, the puppy could attack.

Does you Puppy Need a Mate?

With all of this talk about socialising and avoiding situations with other dogs and puppies, you may be wondering whether it is necessary for your puppy to have a mate. (See also Chapter 1).

This is your choice. Yes, it is true that dogs are instinctively pack animals and prefer to live in packs, but you and your family are part of your puppy's pack.

Providing you follow the basic rules for rearing a well-adjusted puppy as mentioned in Chapters 2, 3, and 5, there is no need to add another puppy to the family unless you really want one.

On the other hand, if you spend a great deal of time away from the house and your puppy doesn't like spending that time alone, another puppy or mature dog of the opposite sex and of similar size, might be a good idea.

If you do decide to get another puppy, be sure to follow the procedure set out in Chapter 1.

Preventing Phobias

There appears to be many dogs nowadays with phobias about fireworks and storms. This problem can occur with puppies that are not familiar with these sounds. They are not everyday occurrences, so the puppy cannot identify them and consequently becomes fearful.

The best way to prevent problems is to accustom your puppy from an early age to as many sounds and experiences as possible. All introductions to new experiences or sounds should be conducted gradually and with the puppy on leash.

How you handle the phobias when they surface is just as important as the desensitisation. You must try not to comfort a fearful puppy. To feel secure, your puppy needs to know you are a strong leader. Coddling only reinforces your puppy's fear.

You can help your puppy learn to tolerate certain sounds. Place your puppy in its portable den and play recordings of many different sounds. Start with the volume at a low level and gradually increase it over time.

Bark Busters do recommend several products that help with this, so speak to your local Bark Busters trainer who will be able to assess your puppy's temperament and assist you to find the correct solution to your puppy's phobia at www.barkbusters.com.au.

Exercising Your Puppy...Brains or Brawn?

There are many opinions about how much exercise puppies require. The common misunderstanding is that exercise will defeat boredom and stave off common doggy problems.

Nothing could be further from the truth. If you want to defeat boredom and associated problems, you must utilize and exercise your puppy's brain, not its brawn.

Puppies tire more quickly when they are performing obedience exercises or activities where they have to use their brain. When they are only performing physically, they can play longer before becoming tired, and their recuperation period is shorter. Since the energy of a young puppy is limited (and increases as it grows), it makes sense that obedience exercises that encourage brain activity take priority over physical exercise. With the limited window of opportunity for education, physical exercise can be saved for those times in between education sessions.

Very young puppies do not need a lot of physical exercise. Puppies are healthier and happier if their exercise is minimized; they can use their nutrition to promote steady, strong growth and development, rather than to sustain excessive exercise.

We are often horrified to see the owners of tiny puppies walking the streets with their puppies in tow. Placing unnecessary stress on soft, immature ligaments can lead to dislocated joints and skeletal damage. Walking a puppy before it has had all its shots also puts it in danger of contracting serious diseases such as parvovirus, rabies, distemper, or kennel cough.

Puppies should not be walked for any distance until they are at least six months old and then only to the puppy's limited capabilities. Fitness needs to build up over time because a puppy's bones are very small and easily fractured.

Puppies should not be encouraged to jump from chairs to the floor, or out of a car until they are well over 12 months of age. Great Danes and similar large breeds should not be permitted to jump until they are well over 2 years of age.

A simple way to break a puppy's fall is to place your right arm across the puppy's chest and take all of the shock of the jump on to your arm, letting the puppy down gradually.

Toys that exercise your puppy's brain, such as the Game Changer ® and the Buster Cube, are great tools to keep an active puppy occupied.

Worming

Puppies and dogs need regular working to protect them from roundworms, hookworms, and tapeworms that can live in their system. Many medications are available.

Puppies (which can be born with worms) are dewormed more frequently than full-grown dogs, who need deworming only every three months. Speak to your veterinarian about the most effective medications to use. When deworming your puppy or dog, deworm the rest of the family pets at the same time.

Six Steps to Being a Responsible Dog Owner

1. Exercise your dog's brain as well as its body.

2. Practice sensible socialisation from puppyhood.

3. Worm your dog regularly. Speak to your vet about deworming and healthcare.

4. Register and microchip. Your vet will advise you – also check out WaggTagg ™ ID Tags by speaking to your local Bark Busters therapist.

5. Provide your puppy with safe and non-toxic toys for entertainment.

6. Provide ongoing education and praise.

Chapter 15

Special Tips for Puppy Owners

Your environment can play a role in your puppy's health and well-being.

Slippery Floors

Tiles, stairs, and uneven territory can affect the skeletal alignment of your puppy and create future health problems. So, limit your puppy's access to stairs and slippery floors.

Stairs

Stairs can create problems for very young dogs as well as for short-haired or long-backed dogs. The constant running up and down the stairs can cause back and shoulder problems. Stairs should be blocked off to prevent the overtaxing that running up and down would cause. If you need to take your puppy upstairs regularly, put it on lead and do not allow it to go up and down the stairs. Walk with it slowly, ensuring that it executes the stairs in a sensible fashion.

Rough Play

If allowing your puppy to play with other puppies, be sure to closely monitor their behaviour, as some puppies can hurt soft natured pups when they play. A gentle natured puppy can suffer long term trauma if injured or frightened during play, something that can result in future aggression towards other dogs as they grow and mature.

Always monitor 'play' between puppies and dogs, keeping them on leash is a good way to avoid the amount of trauma that a soft-natured puppy would experience.

Chapter 16

Summing Up

In summary, be sure to select the right puppy for your lifestyle and choose a reputable breeder or animal shelter. Follow the Seven Steps to Acquiring a New Puppy in Chapter 1.

Remember that your puppy learns from experience and association. You must show it what your want; it cannot be told.

Use the basic steps of communication (Eight Step Sliding Scale for Refocusing in Chapter 3), starting out with the low-growled "Bah" and only escalating to the higher levels if and when required.

Be aware that you are responsible for what your puppy learns. Your puppy needs guidance and careful common-sense education.

Remember to behave like your puppy's leader, consistently educating and rewarding your puppy with praise and encouragement. Provide toys, amusement, shelter, and proper nutrition.

If you have children in the family, follow the eight steps discussed in Chapter 10 to ensure that your dog respects all children in the household.

Be mindful that no child under 12 years of age should be allowed to decide what behaviours are right or wrong for your dog or puppy. Children should never be left alone with the puppy or dog.

To be a responsible dog owner, you must ensure that your dog/puppy is educated, entertained, fed correctly, under your effective control at all times, and registered, immunized, and identifiable by a microchip.

Key Points to Remember

- Ensure that your yard is dog friendly.
- Select the right breed for your personality.
- Select the right temperament.
- Visit your vet for the microchip, vaccinations, and all of your puppy's health needs.
- Decide on the right sleeping quarters for the new puppy.
- Provide leadership, entertainment, good quality nutrition, and adequate shelter.
- Research canine nutrition.
- Seek advice about registration, microchipping, and Bark Busters WaggTagg ™.
- Remember that male and female puppies have different toileting habits.
- Bark Busters system is dog-friendly and is based on the way dogs naturally communicate.
- Use the proper body language, voice tones, and guttural sounds to communicate with your puppy.
- Timing and scene setting are important.
- Good signs of cooperation are good signs. Avoid causing fear.
- Use the recommended sliding scale of refocusing when addressing your puppy's mistakes.
- Hands off! Don't be physical, don't hit or pick up your puppy to control it.
- Children under 12 years must not be left full responsibility for a dog's education.

- When calling your puppy to you, crouch down and stand your ground. Do not chase it.
- A puppy playpen is a vital piece of equipment and will save you a lot of money in the long term.
- Teach your puppy how to behave when being groomed before taking it to a professional establishment.
- It is not absolutely necessary for puppies and dogs to fraternize. They should be taught just to tolerate dogs they meet in the street. If you are going to attend a 'doggy park', wait until after your puppy has reached maturity.

By using this book as your guide and reference, you have an opportunity to select the right puppy that will better match your personality and your lifestyle. This book provides you with the information to mold your puppy's behaviour as it grows and matures, helping it to grow into a calm well behaved dog, one that we believe will make you proud!

By following the philosophy here, you can become your dog's best friend and then truly experience 'Puppy Love'.

Bark Busters Dog Training

Your Bark Busters trainer is ready and willing to assist and advise you about any aspect of dog psychology / behaviour, early puppy education, and proper puppy management in the comfort of your own home.

Go to page 107 for your nearest Bark Busters Trainer contact information.

Chapter 17

Bark Busters 50 Most Popular Breeds

There are hundreds of wonderful dog breeds in the world, all with special attributes. The breeds mentioned here are Bark Busters' 50 most popular breeds according to our training records. The majority of these breeds are also among some of the easiest to educate and train.

Airedale
Australian Cattle Dog
Australian Shepherd
Bearded Collie
Bichon Frise
Border Collie
Boston Terrier
Bull Terrier
Cairn Terrier
Cavalier King Charles
Chihuahua
Clumber Spaniel
Corgi
Dachshund (longhaired)
Doberman
English Springer Spaniel
Flat-coated Retriever
French Bulldog
German Collie
German Shepherd
German Shorthaired
Golden Retriever
Greyhound
Hungarian Vizla
Italian Greyhound

Jack Russell
Kerry Blue
Labrador Retriever
Large Munsterlander
Miniature Pinscher
Nova Scotia Duck
Tolling Retriever
Pointer
Pomeranian
Poodle
Pug
Rottweiler
Rough Collie
Samoyeds
Schippinsterke
Schnauzer
Shetland
Siberian Husky
Skye Terrier
Staffordshire Terrier
Terrier
Tibetan Spaniel
Welsh Springer Spaniel
West Highland White
Whippet

How to Find your Local Bark Busters Trainer

Australia
1800-067-710   www.barkbusters.com.au

Canada
1 866-418-4584   www.barkbusters.ca

Japan
0120-272-109   www.barkbusters.co.jp.com

New Zealand
0800-167-710   www.barkbusters.co.nz

Spain
900-649-022   www.barkbusters.es/en

United States
1-877-280-7100   www.barkbusters.com

United Kingdom
0808-100-4071   www.barkbusters.co.uk